MOONPEAK™

PUBLISHERS

HUNTING JOURNAL

CASE OF EMERGENCY

HUNTER DETAILS

OWNER NAME	
FULL ADDRESS	
EMAIL & NUMBER	
EMERGENCY CONTACT	
EMERGENCY NUMBER	
DOCTOR DETAILS	

INCIDENT DETAILS

If found please return this

HUNTING

LOG BOOK

to:

_____

_____

LOCATION		DATE	
START TIME			
HUNTING TYPE		/ /	

TEMPERATURE		WIND SPEED	
FLORA TYPE		WIND DIRECTION	

WEATHER CONDITION	☀ ☁ ❄ ⛈ 💨	TIME OF YEAR	🌷 ☀ 🍃 ❄

HOURS HUNTED	🕐	HUMIDITY	☀ / 💧
TIME CAUGHT			

TARGET SEX	⚥	TERRAIN LEVEL	1 2 3 4 5

HUNTING PARTY NAMES

WEAPONS/AMMO / EQUIPMENT/TOOLS

■	■
■	■
■	■
■	■

SIGHTINGS & ACTIVITY

FURTHER NOTES & OBSERVATIONS

LOCATION		DATE	
START TIME			
HUNTING TYPE		/ /	

TEMPERATURE		WIND SPEED		
FLORA TYPE		WIND DIRECTION		

WEATHER CONDITION	☀ ☁ ❄ ⛈ 🌬	TIME OF YEAR	🌷 ☀ 🍂 ❄

HOURS HUNTED	🕐	HUMIDITY	☀ / 💧
TIME CAUGHT			

TARGET SEX	⚥	TERRAIN LEVEL	1 2 3 4 5

HUNTING PARTY NAMES

WEAPONS/AMMO | EQUIPMENT/TOOLS

WEAPONS/AMMO	EQUIPMENT/TOOLS
■	■
■	■
■	■
■	■

SIGHTINGS & ACTIVITY

FURTHER NOTES & OBSERVATIONS

LOCATION		DATE	
START TIME			
HUNTING TYPE		/ /	

TEMPERATURE		WIND SPEED		
FLORA TYPE		WIND DIRECTION		

WEATHER CONDITION	☀ ☁ ❄ ⛈ 〰	TIME OF YEAR	🌷 ☀ 🍃 ❄

HOURS HUNTED	🕐	HUMIDITY	☀ / 💧
TIME CAUGHT			

TARGET SEX	⚥	TERRAIN LEVEL	1 2 3 4 5

HUNTING PARTY NAMES

WEAPONS/AMMO · EQUIPMENT/TOOLS

WEAPONS/AMMO	EQUIPMENT/TOOLS
■	■
■	■
■	■
■	■

SIGHTINGS & ACTIVITY

FURTHER NOTES & OBSERVATIONS

LOCATION		DATE	
START TIME			
HUNTING TYPE		/	/

TEMPERATURE						WIND SPEED		
FLORA TYPE						WIND DIRECTION		

WEATHER CONDITION	☀	☁	❄	⛈	💨	TIME OF YEAR	🌷	☀	🍂	❄

HOURS HUNTED	⏰		HUMIDITY	
TIME CAUGHT				

TARGET SEX	⚥		TERRAIN LEVEL	1	2	3	4	5

HUNTING PARTY NAMES

WEAPONS/AMMO | EQUIPMENT/TOOLS

WEAPONS/AMMO	EQUIPMENT/TOOLS
■	■
■	■
■	■
■	■

SIGHTINGS & ACTIVITY

FURTHER NOTES & OBSERVATIONS

LOCATION		DATE	
START TIME			
HUNTING TYPE		/ /	

TEMPERATURE					WIND SPEED	⇒					
FLORA TYPE					WIND DIRECTION						
WEATHER CONDITION	☀	☁	❄	⚡	⇒	TIME OF YEAR	🌷	☀	🍁	❄	
HOURS HUNTED	🕐					HUMIDITY	☀ / 💧				
TIME CAUGHT											
TARGET SEX	⚥					TERRAIN LEVEL	1	2	3	4	5

HUNTING PARTY NAMES

WEAPONS/AMMO	EQUIPMENT/TOOLS
■	■
■	■
■	■
■	■

SIGHTINGS & ACTIVITY

FURTHER NOTES & OBSERVATIONS

LOCATION		DATE	
START TIME			
HUNTING TYPE		/ /	

TEMPERATURE		WIND SPEED	
FLORA TYPE		WIND DIRECTION	
WEATHER CONDITION	☀ ☁ ❄ ⛈ 💨	TIME OF YEAR	🌷 ☀ 🍃 ❄
HOURS HUNTED	🕐	HUMIDITY	
TIME CAUGHT			
TARGET SEX	⚥	TERRAIN LEVEL	1 2 3 4 5

HUNTING PARTY NAMES

WEAPONS/AMMO | EQUIPMENT/TOOLS

WEAPONS/AMMO	EQUIPMENT/TOOLS
■	■
■	■
■	■
■	■

SIGHTINGS & ACTIVITY

FURTHER NOTES & OBSERVATIONS

LOCATION		DATE	
START TIME			
HUNTING TYPE		/ /	

TEMPERATURE		WIND SPEED	
FLORA TYPE		WIND DIRECTION	

WEATHER CONDITION	☀ ☁ ❄ ⛈ 🌬	TIME OF YEAR	🌷 ☀ 🍃 ❄

HOURS HUNTED	🕐	HUMIDITY	☀ / 💧
TIME CAUGHT			

TARGET SEX	⚥	TERRAIN LEVEL	1 2 3 4 5

HUNTING PARTY NAMES

WEAPONS/AMMO · EQUIPMENT/TOOLS

■	■
■	■
■	■
■	■

SIGHTINGS & ACTIVITY

FURTHER NOTES & OBSERVATIONS

LOCATION		DATE	
START TIME			
HUNTING TYPE		/ /	

TEMPERATURE		WIND SPEED	
FLORA TYPE		WIND DIRECTION	

WEATHER CONDITION	☀ ☁ ❄ ⛈ 〰	TIME OF YEAR	🌷 ☀ 🍃 ❄

HOURS HUNTED		HUMIDITY	
TIME CAUGHT			

TARGET SEX	⚥	TERRAIN LEVEL	1 2 3 4 5

HUNTING PARTY NAMES

WEAPONS/AMMO | EQUIPMENT/TOOLS

WEAPONS/AMMO	EQUIPMENT/TOOLS
■	■
■	■
■	■
■	■

SIGHTINGS & ACTIVITY

FURTHER NOTES & OBSERVATIONS

LOCATION		DATE
START TIME		
HUNTING TYPE		/ /

TEMPERATURE		WIND SPEED		
FLORA TYPE		WIND DIRECTION		

WEATHER CONDITION	☀ ☂ ❄ ⛈ 〰	TIME OF YEAR	🌷 ☀ 🍂 ❄

HOURS HUNTED	🕐	HUMIDITY	☀/💧
TIME CAUGHT			

TARGET SEX	⚥	TERRAIN LEVEL	1 2 3 4 5

HUNTING PARTY NAMES

WEAPONS/AMMO | EQUIPMENT/TOOLS

WEAPONS/AMMO	EQUIPMENT/TOOLS
■	■
■	■
■	■
■	■

SIGHTINGS & ACTIVITY

FURTHER NOTES & OBSERVATIONS

LOCATION		DATE	
START TIME			
HUNTING TYPE		/ /	

TEMPERATURE		WIND SPEED		
FLORA TYPE		WIND DIRECTION		

WEATHER CONDITION	☀ ☁ ❄ ⛈ 🌬	TIME OF YEAR	🌷 ☀ 🍃 ❄

HOURS HUNTED	🕐	HUMIDITY	☀ / 💧
TIME CAUGHT			

TARGET SEX	⚥	TERRAIN LEVEL	1 2 3 4 5

HUNTING PARTY NAMES

WEAPONS/AMMO EQUIPMENT/TOOLS

WEAPONS/AMMO	EQUIPMENT/TOOLS
■	■
■	■
■	■
■	■

SIGHTINGS & ACTIVITY

FURTHER NOTES & OBSERVATIONS

LOCATION		DATE		
START TIME				
HUNTING TYPE		/ /		

TEMPERATURE					WIND SPEED					
FLORA TYPE					WIND DIRECTION					
WEATHER CONDITION	☀	☁	❄	⛈	➥	TIME OF YEAR	🌷	☀	🍁	❄
HOURS HUNTED	🕐					HUMIDITY	☀/💧			
TIME CAUGHT										
TARGET SEX	⚥					TERRAIN LEVEL	1	2	3 4 5	

HUNTING PARTY NAMES

WEAPONS/AMMO	EQUIPMENT/TOOLS
■	■
■	■
■	■
■	■

SIGHTINGS & ACTIVITY

FURTHER NOTES & OBSERVATIONS

LOCATION		DATE	
START TIME			
HUNTING TYPE		/ /	

TEMPERATURE		WIND SPEED	
FLORA TYPE		WIND DIRECTION	

WEATHER CONDITION	☀ ☁ ❄ ⛈ 🌬	TIME OF YEAR	🌷 ☀ 🍃 ❄

HOURS HUNTED	🕐	HUMIDITY	☀ / 💧
TIME CAUGHT			

TARGET SEX	⚥	TERRAIN LEVEL	1 2 3 4 5

HUNTING PARTY NAMES

WEAPONS/AMMO — EQUIPMENT/TOOLS

WEAPONS/AMMO	EQUIPMENT/TOOLS
■	■
■	■
■	■
■	■

SIGHTINGS & ACTIVITY

FURTHER NOTES & OBSERVATIONS

LOCATION		DATE		
START TIME				
HUNTING TYPE		/ /		

TEMPERATURE		WIND SPEED		
FLORA TYPE		WIND DIRECTION		

| WEATHER CONDITION | ☀ ☁ ❄ ⛈ 🌬 | TIME OF YEAR | 🌷 ☀ 🍃 ❄ |

HOURS HUNTED	🕐	HUMIDITY	☀ / 💧
TIME CAUGHT			

| TARGET SEX | ⚥ | TERRAIN LEVEL | 1 2 3 4 5 |

HUNTING PARTY NAMES

WEAPONS/AMMO | EQUIPMENT/TOOLS

WEAPONS/AMMO	EQUIPMENT/TOOLS
▪	▪
▪	▪
▪	▪
▪	▪

SIGHTINGS & ACTIVITY

FURTHER NOTES & OBSERVATIONS

LOCATION		DATE
START TIME		
HUNTING TYPE		/ /

TEMPERATURE		WIND SPEED		
FLORA TYPE		WIND DIRECTION		

WEATHER CONDITION	☀ ☁ ❄ ⚡ 🌬	TIME OF YEAR	🌷 ☀ 🍃 ❄

HOURS HUNTED	🕐	HUMIDITY	
TIME CAUGHT			

TARGET SEX	⚥	TERRAIN LEVEL	1 2 3 4 5

HUNTING PARTY NAMES

WEAPONS/AMMO EQUIPMENT/TOOLS

WEAPONS/AMMO	EQUIPMENT/TOOLS
■	■
■	■
■	■
■	■

SIGHTINGS & ACTIVITY

FURTHER NOTES & OBSERVATIONS

LOCATION		DATE	
START TIME			
HUNTING TYPE		/ /	

TEMPERATURE		WIND SPEED		
FLORA TYPE		WIND DIRECTION		

WEATHER CONDITION	☀ ☁ ❄ ⛈ 💨	TIME OF YEAR	🌷 ☀ 🍂 ❄

HOURS HUNTED	🕐	HUMIDITY	☀ / 💧
TIME CAUGHT			

TARGET SEX	⚥	TERRAIN LEVEL	1 2 3 4 5

HUNTING PARTY NAMES

WEAPONS/AMMO / EQUIPMENT/TOOLS

WEAPONS/AMMO	EQUIPMENT/TOOLS
■	■
■	■
■	■
■	■

SIGHTINGS & ACTIVITY

FURTHER NOTES & OBSERVATIONS

LOCATION		DATE	
START TIME			
HUNTING TYPE		/ /	

TEMPERATURE		WIND SPEED	
FLORA TYPE		WIND DIRECTION	

WEATHER CONDITION	☀ ☁ ❄ ⛈ 🌬	TIME OF YEAR	🌷 ☀ 🍃 ❄

HOURS HUNTED	🕐	HUMIDITY	☀ / 💧
TIME CAUGHT			

TARGET SEX	⚥	TERRAIN LEVEL	1 2 3 4 5

HUNTING PARTY NAMES

WEAPONS/AMMO | ## EQUIPMENT/TOOLS

WEAPONS/AMMO	EQUIPMENT/TOOLS
■	■
■	■
■	■
■	■

SIGHTINGS & ACTIVITY

FURTHER NOTES & OBSERVATIONS

LOCATION		DATE		
START TIME				
HUNTING TYPE		/ /		

TEMPERATURE		WIND SPEED	🌬	
FLORA TYPE		WIND DIRECTION		

WEATHER CONDITION	🌞 ☁ ❄ ⛈ 🌬	TIME OF YEAR	🌷 🌞 🍁 ❄

HOURS HUNTED	🕐	HUMIDITY	🌞 / 💧
TIME CAUGHT			

TARGET SEX	⚧	TERRAIN LEVEL	1 2 3 4 5

HUNTING PARTY NAMES

WEAPONS/AMMO | EQUIPMENT/TOOLS

■	■
■	■
■	■
■	■

SIGHTINGS & ACTIVITY

FURTHER NOTES & OBSERVATIONS

LOCATION		DATE	
START TIME			
HUNTING TYPE		/ /	

TEMPERATURE		WIND SPEED	⇒	
FLORA TYPE		WIND DIRECTION		

WEATHER CONDITION	☀ ☁ ❄ ⛈ ⇒	TIME OF YEAR	🌷 ☀ 🍂 ❄

HOURS HUNTED	🕐	HUMIDITY	☀ / 💧
TIME CAUGHT			

TARGET SEX	⚥	TERRAIN LEVEL	1 2 3 4 5

HUNTING PARTY NAMES

WEAPONS/AMMO

EQUIPMENT/TOOLS

WEAPONS/AMMO	EQUIPMENT/TOOLS
■	■
■	■
■	■
■	■

SIGHTINGS & ACTIVITY

FURTHER NOTES & OBSERVATIONS

LOCATION		DATE
START TIME		
HUNTING TYPE		/ /

TEMPERATURE						WIND SPEED		
FLORA TYPE						WIND DIRECTION		

WEATHER CONDITION	☀	☁	❄	⛈	⇌	TIME OF YEAR	🌷	☀	🍃	❄	

HOURS HUNTED	🕐		HUMIDITY	
TIME CAUGHT				

TARGET SEX	⚤		TERRAIN LEVEL	1	2	3	4	5

HUNTING PARTY NAMES

WEAPONS/AMMO / EQUIPMENT/TOOLS

WEAPONS/AMMO	EQUIPMENT/TOOLS
■	■
■	■
■	■
■	■

SIGHTINGS & ACTIVITY

FURTHER NOTES & OBSERVATIONS

LOCATION		DATE	
START TIME			
HUNTING TYPE		/ /	

TEMPERATURE		WIND SPEED	
FLORA TYPE		WIND DIRECTION	

WEATHER CONDITION	☀ ☁ ❄ ⛈ 💨	TIME OF YEAR	🌷 ☀ 🍃 ❄

HOURS HUNTED	🕐	HUMIDITY	☀ / 💧
TIME CAUGHT			

TARGET SEX	⚥	TERRAIN LEVEL	1 2 3 4 5

HUNTING PARTY NAMES

WEAPONS/AMMO · EQUIPMENT/TOOLS

WEAPONS/AMMO	EQUIPMENT/TOOLS
■	■
■	■
■	■
■	■

SIGHTINGS & ACTIVITY

FURTHER NOTES & OBSERVATIONS

LOCATION		DATE	
START TIME			
HUNTING TYPE		/ /	

TEMPERATURE		WIND SPEED	
FLORA TYPE		WIND DIRECTION	

WEATHER CONDITION	☀ ☁ ❄ ⛈ 🌬	TIME OF YEAR	🌷 ☀ 🍂 ❄

HOURS HUNTED	🕐	HUMIDITY	
TIME CAUGHT			

TARGET SEX	⚥	TERRAIN LEVEL	1 2 3 4 5

HUNTING PARTY NAMES

WEAPONS/AMMO

EQUIPMENT/TOOLS

- ■
- ■
- ■
- ■

- ■
- ■
- ■
- ■

SIGHTINGS & ACTIVITY

FURTHER NOTES & OBSERVATIONS

LOCATION		DATE	
START TIME			
HUNTING TYPE		/	/

TEMPERATURE		WIND SPEED			
FLORA TYPE		WIND DIRECTION			

WEATHER CONDITION	☀ ☁ ❄ ⛈ 🌬	TIME OF YEAR	🌷 ☀ 🍃 ❄

HOURS HUNTED	🕐	HUMIDITY	☀ / 💧
TIME CAUGHT			

TARGET SEX	⚥	TERRAIN LEVEL	1 2 3 4 5

HUNTING PARTY NAMES

WEAPONS/AMMO · EQUIPMENT/TOOLS

WEAPONS/AMMO	EQUIPMENT/TOOLS
■	■
■	■
■	■
■	■

SIGHTINGS & ACTIVITY

FURTHER NOTES & OBSERVATIONS

LOCATION		DATE	
START TIME			
HUNTING TYPE		/ /	

TEMPERATURE		WIND SPEED	
FLORA TYPE		WIND DIRECTION	

WEATHER CONDITION	☀ ☁ ❄ ⛈ 💨	TIME OF YEAR	🌷 ☀ 🍂 ❄

HOURS HUNTED		HUMIDITY	
TIME CAUGHT			

TARGET SEX	⚥	TERRAIN LEVEL	1 2 3 4 5

HUNTING PARTY NAMES

WEAPONS/AMMO | EQUIPMENT/TOOLS

■	■
■	■
■	■
■	■

SIGHTINGS & ACTIVITY

FURTHER NOTES & OBSERVATIONS

LOCATION		DATE	
START TIME			
HUNTING TYPE		/ /	

TEMPERATURE					WIND SPEED	⇌					
FLORA TYPE					WIND DIRECTION						
WEATHER CONDITION	☀	☁	❄	⚡	⇌	TIME OF YEAR	🌷	☀	🍃	❄	
HOURS HUNTED	🕐					HUMIDITY	☀ / 💧				
TIME CAUGHT											
TARGET SEX	⚥					TERRAIN LEVEL	1	2	3	4	5

HUNTING PARTY NAMES

WEAPONS/AMMO | EQUIPMENT/TOOLS

WEAPONS/AMMO	EQUIPMENT/TOOLS
■	■
■	■
■	■
■	■

SIGHTINGS & ACTIVITY

FURTHER NOTES & OBSERVATIONS

LOCATION		DATE	
START TIME			
HUNTING TYPE		/ /	

TEMPERATURE		WIND SPEED	⇌	
FLORA TYPE		WIND DIRECTION		

WEATHER CONDITION	☀ ☁ ❄ ⛈ ⇌	TIME OF YEAR	🌷 ☀ 🍃 ❄

HOURS HUNTED	🕐	HUMIDITY	☀/💧
TIME CAUGHT			

TARGET SEX	⚤	TERRAIN LEVEL	1 2 3 4 5

HUNTING PARTY NAMES

WEAPONS/AMMO · EQUIPMENT/TOOLS

WEAPONS/AMMO	EQUIPMENT/TOOLS
■	■
■	■
■	■
■	■

SIGHTINGS & ACTIVITY

FURTHER NOTES & OBSERVATIONS

LOCATION		DATE
START TIME		
HUNTING TYPE		/ /

TEMPERATURE		WIND SPEED		
FLORA TYPE		WIND DIRECTION		

WEATHER CONDITION	☀ ☁ ❄ ⛈ 💨	TIME OF YEAR	🌷 ☀ 🍃 ❄

HOURS HUNTED	🕐	HUMIDITY	☀ / 💧
TIME CAUGHT			

TARGET SEX	⚥	TERRAIN LEVEL	1 2 3 4 5

HUNTING PARTY NAMES

WEAPONS/AMMO | EQUIPMENT/TOOLS

WEAPONS/AMMO	EQUIPMENT/TOOLS
■	■
■	■
■	■
■	■

SIGHTINGS & ACTIVITY

FURTHER NOTES & OBSERVATIONS

LOCATION		DATE	
START TIME			
HUNTING TYPE		/ /	

TEMPERATURE		WIND SPEED	
FLORA TYPE		WIND DIRECTION	

WEATHER CONDITION	☀ ☁ ❄ ⛈ 🌬	TIME OF YEAR	🌷 ☀ 🍂 ❄
HOURS HUNTED	🕐	HUMIDITY	☀ / 💧
TIME CAUGHT			
TARGET SEX	⚥	TERRAIN LEVEL	1 2 3 4 5

HUNTING PARTY NAMES

WEAPONS/AMMO	EQUIPMENT/TOOLS
■	■
■	■
■	■
■	■

SIGHTINGS & ACTIVITY

FURTHER NOTES & OBSERVATIONS

LOCATION		DATE	
START TIME			
HUNTING TYPE		/ /	

TEMPERATURE		WIND SPEED		
FLORA TYPE		WIND DIRECTION		

WEATHER CONDITION	☀ ☁ ❄ ⛈ 💨	TIME OF YEAR	🌷 ☀ 🍃 ❄

HOURS HUNTED	🕐	HUMIDITY	
TIME CAUGHT			

TARGET SEX	⚥	TERRAIN LEVEL	1 2 3 4 5

HUNTING PARTY NAMES

WEAPONS/AMMO | ## EQUIPMENT/TOOLS

WEAPONS/AMMO	EQUIPMENT/TOOLS
▪	▪
▪	▪
▪	▪
▪	▪

SIGHTINGS & ACTIVITY

FURTHER NOTES & OBSERVATIONS

LOCATION		DATE		
START TIME				
HUNTING TYPE		/ /		

TEMPERATURE		WIND SPEED		
FLORA TYPE		WIND DIRECTION		

WEATHER CONDITION	☀ ☁ ❄ ⛈ 💨	TIME OF YEAR	🌷 ☀ 🍂 ❄

HOURS HUNTED	🕐	HUMIDITY	☀ / ○
TIME CAUGHT			

TARGET SEX	⚥	TERRAIN LEVEL	1 2 3 4 5

HUNTING PARTY NAMES

WEAPONS/AMMO | EQUIPMENT/TOOLS

■	■
■	■
■	■
■	■

SIGHTINGS & ACTIVITY

FURTHER NOTES & OBSERVATIONS

LOCATION		DATE	
START TIME			
HUNTING TYPE		/ /	

TEMPERATURE		WIND SPEED	
FLORA TYPE		WIND DIRECTION	

WEATHER CONDITION	☀ ☁ ❄ ⛈ 🌬	TIME OF YEAR	🌷 ☀ 🍃 ❄

HOURS HUNTED	🕐	HUMIDITY	
TIME CAUGHT			

TARGET SEX	⚥	TERRAIN LEVEL	1 2 3 4 5

HUNTING PARTY NAMES

WEAPONS/AMMO | EQUIPMENT/TOOLS

WEAPONS/AMMO	EQUIPMENT/TOOLS
▪	▪
▪	▪
▪	▪
▪	▪

SIGHTINGS & ACTIVITY

FURTHER NOTES & OBSERVATIONS

LOCATION		DATE	
START TIME			
HUNTING TYPE		/ /	

TEMPERATURE		WIND SPEED		
FLORA TYPE		WIND DIRECTION		

WEATHER CONDITION	☀ ☁ ❄ ⛈ 🌬	TIME OF YEAR	🌷 ☀ 🍃 ❄

HOURS HUNTED	🕐	HUMIDITY	☀ / 💧
TIME CAUGHT			

TARGET SEX	⚥	TERRAIN LEVEL	1 2 3 4 5

HUNTING PARTY NAMES

WEAPONS/AMMO | EQUIPMENT/TOOLS

WEAPONS/AMMO	EQUIPMENT/TOOLS
■	■
■	■
■	■
■	■

SIGHTINGS & ACTIVITY

FURTHER NOTES & OBSERVATIONS

LOCATION		DATE	
START TIME			
HUNTING TYPE		/ /	

TEMPERATURE		WIND SPEED	
FLORA TYPE		WIND DIRECTION	

WEATHER CONDITION	☀ ☁ ❄ ⛈ 🌬	TIME OF YEAR	🌷 ☀ 🍃 ❄

HOURS HUNTED	🕐	HUMIDITY	☀ / 💧
TIME CAUGHT			

TARGET SEX	⚥	TERRAIN LEVEL	1 2 3 4 5

HUNTING PARTY NAMES

WEAPONS/AMMO — EQUIPMENT/TOOLS

WEAPONS/AMMO	EQUIPMENT/TOOLS
■	■
■	■
■	■
■	■

SIGHTINGS & ACTIVITY

FURTHER NOTES & OBSERVATIONS

LOCATION		DATE		
START TIME				
HUNTING TYPE			/	/

TEMPERATURE		WIND SPEED		
FLORA TYPE		WIND DIRECTION		

WEATHER CONDITION	☀ ☁ ❄ ⛈ 🌬	TIME OF YEAR	🌷 ☀ 🍂 ❄		

HOURS HUNTED	🕐	HUMIDITY	☀ / 💧		
TIME CAUGHT					

TARGET SEX	⚥	TERRAIN LEVEL	1 2 3 4 5		

HUNTING PARTY NAMES

WEAPONS/AMMO   EQUIPMENT/TOOLS

■	■
■	■
■	■
■	■

SIGHTINGS & ACTIVITY

FURTHER NOTES & OBSERVATIONS

LOCATION		DATE	
START TIME			
HUNTING TYPE		/ /	

TEMPERATURE		WIND SPEED		
FLORA TYPE		WIND DIRECTION		

WEATHER CONDITION	☀ ☁ ❄ ⛈ 🌬	TIME OF YEAR	🌷 ☀ 🍃 ❄

HOURS HUNTED	🕐	HUMIDITY	☀ / 💧
TIME CAUGHT			

TARGET SEX	⚥	TERRAIN LEVEL	1 2 3 4 5

HUNTING PARTY NAMES

WEAPONS/AMMO | EQUIPMENT/TOOLS

WEAPONS/AMMO	EQUIPMENT/TOOLS
■	■
■	■
■	■
■	■

SIGHTINGS & ACTIVITY

FURTHER NOTES & OBSERVATIONS

LOCATION		DATE		
START TIME				
HUNTING TYPE		/	/	

TEMPERATURE		WIND SPEED	⇉	
FLORA TYPE		WIND DIRECTION		

WEATHER CONDITION	☀ ☁ ❄ ⚡ ⇉	TIME OF YEAR	🌷 ☀ 🍁 ❄

HOURS HUNTED	🕐	HUMIDITY	☀/💧
TIME CAUGHT			

TARGET SEX	⚥	TERRAIN LEVEL	1 2 3 4 5

HUNTING PARTY NAMES

WEAPONS/AMMO / EQUIPMENT/TOOLS

■	■
■	■
■	■
■	■

SIGHTINGS & ACTIVITY

FURTHER NOTES & OBSERVATIONS

LOCATION		DATE	
START TIME			
HUNTING TYPE		/	/

TEMPERATURE		WIND SPEED		
FLORA TYPE		WIND DIRECTION		

WEATHER CONDITION	☀ ☁ ❄ ⛈ 🌬	TIME OF YEAR	🌷 ☀ 🍂 ❄

HOURS HUNTED	🕐	HUMIDITY	☀ / 💧
TIME CAUGHT			

TARGET SEX	⚥	TERRAIN LEVEL	1 2 3 4 5

HUNTING PARTY NAMES

WEAPONS/AMMO | EQUIPMENT/TOOLS

■	■
■	■
■	■
■	■

SIGHTINGS & ACTIVITY

FURTHER NOTES & OBSERVATIONS

LOCATION		DATE		
START TIME				
HUNTING TYPE		/ /		

TEMPERATURE			WIND SPEED	⇾	
FLORA TYPE			WIND DIRECTION		

WEATHER CONDITION	☀	☁	❄	⛈	⇾	TIME OF YEAR	🌷	☀	🍂	❄	

HOURS HUNTED	🕐		HUMIDITY	☀/💧	
TIME CAUGHT					

TARGET SEX	⚥		TERRAIN LEVEL	1	2	3	4	5

HUNTING PARTY NAMES

WEAPONS/AMMO / EQUIPMENT/TOOLS

WEAPONS/AMMO	EQUIPMENT/TOOLS
■	■
■	■
■	■
■	■

SIGHTINGS & ACTIVITY

FURTHER NOTES & OBSERVATIONS

LOCATION		DATE	
START TIME			
HUNTING TYPE		/ /	

TEMPERATURE			WIND SPEED		
FLORA TYPE			WIND DIRECTION		

WEATHER CONDITION	☀	☁	❄	⛈	≋	TIME OF YEAR	🌷	☀	🍂	❄

HOURS HUNTED	⏱		HUMIDITY	☀	
TIME CAUGHT				💧	

TARGET SEX	⚢		TERRAIN LEVEL	1	2	3	4	5

HUNTING PARTY NAMES

WEAPONS/AMMO | ## EQUIPMENT/TOOLS

■	■
■	■
■	■
■	■

SIGHTINGS & ACTIVITY

FURTHER NOTES & OBSERVATIONS

LOCATION		DATE
START TIME		
HUNTING TYPE		/ /

TEMPERATURE		WIND SPEED		
FLORA TYPE		WIND DIRECTION		

WEATHER CONDITION	☀ ☁ ❄ ⛈ 🌬	TIME OF YEAR	🌷 ☀ 🍃 ❄

HOURS HUNTED	🕐	HUMIDITY	☀ / 💧
TIME CAUGHT			

TARGET SEX	⚥	TERRAIN LEVEL	1 2 3 4 5

HUNTING PARTY NAMES

WEAPONS/AMMO | ## EQUIPMENT/TOOLS

■	■
■	■
■	■
■	■

SIGHTINGS & ACTIVITY

FURTHER NOTES & OBSERVATIONS

LOCATION		DATE	
START TIME			
HUNTING TYPE		/ /	

TEMPERATURE						WIND SPEED					
FLORA TYPE						WIND DIRECTION					
WEATHER CONDITION	☀	☁	❄	⛈	💨	TIME OF YEAR	🌷	☀	🍃	❄	
HOURS HUNTED	🕐					HUMIDITY	☀ 💧				
TIME CAUGHT											
TARGET SEX	⚥					TERRAIN LEVEL	1	2	3	4	5

HUNTING PARTY NAMES

WEAPONS/AMMO | EQUIPMENT/TOOLS

WEAPONS/AMMO	EQUIPMENT/TOOLS
■	■
■	■
■	■
■	■

SIGHTINGS & ACTIVITY

FURTHER NOTES & OBSERVATIONS

LOCATION		DATE	
START TIME			
HUNTING TYPE		/ /	

TEMPERATURE		WIND SPEED		
FLORA TYPE		WIND DIRECTION		

WEATHER CONDITION	☼ ☁ ❄ ⛈ 〰	TIME OF YEAR	🌷 ☀ 🍂 ❄

HOURS HUNTED	🕐	HUMIDITY	☼ / 💧
TIME CAUGHT			

TARGET SEX	⚥	TERRAIN LEVEL	1 2 3 4 5

HUNTING PARTY NAMES

WEAPONS/AMMO | EQUIPMENT/TOOLS

WEAPONS/AMMO	EQUIPMENT/TOOLS
■	■
■	■
■	■
■	■

SIGHTINGS & ACTIVITY

FURTHER NOTES & OBSERVATIONS

LOCATION		DATE	
START TIME			
HUNTING TYPE		/ /	

TEMPERATURE		WIND SPEED		
FLORA TYPE		WIND DIRECTION		

WEATHER CONDITION	☀ ☁ ❄ ⛈ ⇀	TIME OF YEAR	🌷 ☀ 🍁 ❄

HOURS HUNTED	🕐	HUMIDITY	☀ / 💧
TIME CAUGHT			

TARGET SEX	⚥	TERRAIN LEVEL	1 2 3 4 5

HUNTING PARTY NAMES

WEAPONS/AMMO · EQUIPMENT/TOOLS

WEAPONS/AMMO	EQUIPMENT/TOOLS
■	■
■	■
■	■
■	■

SIGHTINGS & ACTIVITY

FURTHER NOTES & OBSERVATIONS

LOCATION		DATE	
START TIME			
HUNTING TYPE		/ /	

TEMPERATURE		WIND SPEED	
FLORA TYPE		WIND DIRECTION	

WEATHER CONDITION	☀ ☁ ❄ ⛈ 🌬	TIME OF YEAR	🌷 ☀ 🍃 ❄

HOURS HUNTED	🕐	HUMIDITY	☀ / 💧
TIME CAUGHT			

TARGET SEX	⚦	TERRAIN LEVEL	1 2 3 4 5

HUNTING PARTY NAMES

WEAPONS/AMMO · EQUIPMENT/TOOLS

WEAPONS/AMMO	EQUIPMENT/TOOLS
■	■
■	■
■	■
■	■

SIGHTINGS & ACTIVITY

FURTHER NOTES & OBSERVATIONS

LOCATION		DATE	
START TIME			
HUNTING TYPE		/ /	

TEMPERATURE		WIND SPEED		
FLORA TYPE		WIND DIRECTION		

WEATHER CONDITION	☀ ☁ ❄ ⛈ 💨	TIME OF YEAR	🌷 ☀ 🍂 ❄

HOURS HUNTED	🕐	HUMIDITY	☀ / 💧
TIME CAUGHT			

TARGET SEX	⚥	TERRAIN LEVEL	1 2 3 4 5

HUNTING PARTY NAMES

WEAPONS/AMMO | EQUIPMENT/TOOLS

WEAPONS/AMMO	EQUIPMENT/TOOLS
■	■
■	■
■	■
■	■

SIGHTINGS & ACTIVITY

FURTHER NOTES & OBSERVATIONS

LOCATION		DATE		
START TIME				
HUNTING TYPE		/	/	

TEMPERATURE		WIND SPEED		
FLORA TYPE		WIND DIRECTION		

WEATHER CONDITION	☀ ☁ ❄ ⛈ 🌬	TIME OF YEAR	🌷 ☀ 🍃 ❄

HOURS HUNTED	🕐	HUMIDITY	☀ / 💧
TIME CAUGHT			

TARGET SEX	⚥	TERRAIN LEVEL	1 2 3 4 5

HUNTING PARTY NAMES

WEAPONS/AMMO · EQUIPMENT/TOOLS

■	■
■	■
■	■
■	■

SIGHTINGS & ACTIVITY

FURTHER NOTES & OBSERVATIONS

LOCATION		DATE	
START TIME			
HUNTING TYPE		/ /	

TEMPERATURE		WIND SPEED	
FLORA TYPE		WIND DIRECTION	

WEATHER CONDITION	☀ ☁ ❄ ⛈ 🌬	TIME OF YEAR	🌷 ☀ 🍃 ❄

HOURS HUNTED	🕐	HUMIDITY	☀ / 💧
TIME CAUGHT			

TARGET SEX	⚥	TERRAIN LEVEL	1 2 3 4 5

HUNTING PARTY NAMES

WEAPONS/AMMO

EQUIPMENT/TOOLS

- ■
- ■
- ■
- ■

- ■
- ■
- ■
- ■

SIGHTINGS & ACTIVITY

FURTHER NOTES & OBSERVATIONS

LOCATION		DATE	
START TIME			
HUNTING TYPE		/ /	

TEMPERATURE		WIND SPEED	≈	
FLORA TYPE		WIND DIRECTION		

WEATHER CONDITION	☀ ☁ ❄ ⛈ ≈	TIME OF YEAR	🌷 ☀ 🍂 ❄

HOURS HUNTED	🕐	HUMIDITY	☀/💧
TIME CAUGHT			

TARGET SEX	⚥	TERRAIN LEVEL	1 2 3 4 5

HUNTING PARTY NAMES

WEAPONS/AMMO · EQUIPMENT/TOOLS

■	■
■	■
■	■
■	■

SIGHTINGS & ACTIVITY

FURTHER NOTES & OBSERVATIONS

LOCATION		DATE	
START TIME			
HUNTING TYPE		/ /	

TEMPERATURE		WIND SPEED	
FLORA TYPE		WIND DIRECTION	

WEATHER CONDITION	☀ ☁ ❄ ⛈ ⇀	TIME OF YEAR	🌷 ☀ 🍃 ❄
HOURS HUNTED / TIME CAUGHT	🕐	HUMIDITY	☀ / 💧
TARGET SEX	⚥	TERRAIN LEVEL	1 2 3 4 5

HUNTING PARTY NAMES

WEAPONS/AMMO — EQUIPMENT/TOOLS

WEAPONS/AMMO	EQUIPMENT/TOOLS
▪	▪
▪	▪
▪	▪
▪	▪

SIGHTINGS & ACTIVITY

FURTHER NOTES & OBSERVATIONS

LOCATION		DATE	
START TIME			
HUNTING TYPE		/ /	

TEMPERATURE		WIND SPEED	
FLORA TYPE		WIND DIRECTION	

WEATHER CONDITION	☀ ☁ ❄ ⛈ 💨	TIME OF YEAR	🌷 ☀ 🍃 ❄

HOURS HUNTED	🕐	HUMIDITY	☀ / 💧
TIME CAUGHT			

TARGET SEX	⚥	TERRAIN LEVEL	1 2 3 4 5

HUNTING PARTY NAMES

WEAPONS/AMMO & EQUIPMENT/TOOLS

WEAPONS/AMMO	EQUIPMENT/TOOLS
■	■
■	■
■	■
■	■

SIGHTINGS & ACTIVITY

FURTHER NOTES & OBSERVATIONS

LOCATION		DATE	
START TIME			
HUNTING TYPE		/ /	

TEMPERATURE		WIND SPEED	
FLORA TYPE		WIND DIRECTION	

WEATHER CONDITION	☀ ☁ ❄ ⛈ 🌬	TIME OF YEAR	🌷 ☀ 🍂 ❄

HOURS HUNTED	🕐	HUMIDITY	
TIME CAUGHT			

TARGET SEX	⚥	TERRAIN LEVEL	1 2 3 4 5

HUNTING PARTY NAMES

WEAPONS/AMMO | EQUIPMENT/TOOLS

WEAPONS/AMMO	EQUIPMENT/TOOLS
■	■
■	■
■	■
■	■

SIGHTINGS & ACTIVITY

FURTHER NOTES & OBSERVATIONS

LOCATION		DATE	
START TIME			
HUNTING TYPE		/ /	

TEMPERATURE		WIND SPEED		
FLORA TYPE		WIND DIRECTION		

WEATHER CONDITION	☀ ☁ ❄ ⛈ 🌬	TIME OF YEAR	🌷 ☀ 🍃 ❄

HOURS HUNTED	🕐	HUMIDITY	☀ / 💧
TIME CAUGHT			

TARGET SEX	⚥	TERRAIN LEVEL	1 2 3 4 5

HUNTING PARTY NAMES

WEAPONS/AMMO | EQUIPMENT/TOOLS

WEAPONS/AMMO	EQUIPMENT/TOOLS
■	■
■	■
■	■
■	■

SIGHTINGS & ACTIVITY

FURTHER NOTES & OBSERVATIONS

LOCATION		DATE	
START TIME			
HUNTING TYPE		/	/

TEMPERATURE		WIND SPEED		
FLORA TYPE		WIND DIRECTION		

WEATHER CONDITION	☀ ☁ ❄ ⛈ 🌬	TIME OF YEAR	🌷 ☀ 🍃 ❄

HOURS HUNTED	🕐	HUMIDITY	
TIME CAUGHT			

TARGET SEX	⚥	TERRAIN LEVEL	1 2 3 4 5

HUNTING PARTY NAMES

WEAPONS/AMMO | EQUIPMENT/TOOLS

WEAPONS/AMMO	EQUIPMENT/TOOLS
■	■
■	■
■	■
■	■

SIGHTINGS & ACTIVITY

FURTHER NOTES & OBSERVATIONS

LOCATION		DATE	
START TIME			
HUNTING TYPE		/ /	

TEMPERATURE		WIND SPEED	
FLORA TYPE		WIND DIRECTION	
WEATHER CONDITION	☀ ☁ ❄ ⛈ 💨	TIME OF YEAR	🌷 ☀ 🍁 ❄
HOURS HUNTED	🕐	HUMIDITY	☀ / 💧
TIME CAUGHT			
TARGET SEX	⚥	TERRAIN LEVEL	1 2 3 4 5

HUNTING PARTY NAMES

WEAPONS/AMMO · EQUIPMENT/TOOLS

WEAPONS/AMMO	EQUIPMENT/TOOLS
■	■
■	■
■	■
■	■

SIGHTINGS & ACTIVITY

FURTHER NOTES & OBSERVATIONS

LOCATION		DATE	
START TIME			
HUNTING TYPE		/ /	

TEMPERATURE		WIND SPEED		
FLORA TYPE		WIND DIRECTION		

WEATHER CONDITION	☀ ☁ ❄ ⛈ 💨	TIME OF YEAR	🌷 ☀ 🍃 ❄

HOURS HUNTED	🕐	HUMIDITY	☀ / 💧
TIME CAUGHT			

TARGET SEX	⚥	TERRAIN LEVEL	1 2 3 4 5

HUNTING PARTY NAMES

WEAPONS/AMMO — EQUIPMENT/TOOLS

WEAPONS/AMMO	EQUIPMENT/TOOLS
■	■
■	■
■	■
■	■

SIGHTINGS & ACTIVITY

FURTHER NOTES & OBSERVATIONS

LOCATION		DATE	
START TIME			
HUNTING TYPE		/ /	

TEMPERATURE		WIND SPEED	
FLORA TYPE		WIND DIRECTION	

WEATHER CONDITION	☀ ☁ ❄ ⛈ 💨	TIME OF YEAR	🌷 ☀ 🍃 ❄

HOURS HUNTED	🕐	HUMIDITY	☀ / 💧
TIME CAUGHT			

TARGET SEX	⚥	TERRAIN LEVEL	1 2 3 4 5

HUNTING PARTY NAMES

WEAPONS/AMMO · EQUIPMENT/TOOLS

■	■
■	■
■	■
■	■

SIGHTINGS & ACTIVITY

FURTHER NOTES & OBSERVATIONS

LOCATION		DATE	
START TIME			
HUNTING TYPE		/ /	

TEMPERATURE		WIND SPEED	
FLORA TYPE		WIND DIRECTION	

WEATHER CONDITION	☀ ☁ ❄ ⛈ 💨	TIME OF YEAR	🌷 ☀ 🍃 ❄

HOURS HUNTED		HUMIDITY	
TIME CAUGHT			

TARGET SEX	⚥	TERRAIN LEVEL	1 2 3 4 5

HUNTING PARTY NAMES

WEAPONS/AMMO

- ■
- ■
- ■
- ■

EQUIPMENT/TOOLS

- ■
- ■
- ■
- ■

SIGHTINGS & ACTIVITY

FURTHER NOTES & OBSERVATIONS

LOCATION		DATE	
START TIME			
HUNTING TYPE		/ /	

TEMPERATURE		WIND SPEED		
FLORA TYPE		WIND DIRECTION		

WEATHER CONDITION	☀ ☁ ❄ ⛈ 🌬	TIME OF YEAR	🌷 ☀ 🍂 ❄

HOURS HUNTED	🕐	HUMIDITY	☀ / 💧
TIME CAUGHT			

TARGET SEX	⚥	TERRAIN LEVEL	1 2 3 4 5

HUNTING PARTY NAMES

WEAPONS/AMMO | EQUIPMENT/TOOLS

WEAPONS/AMMO	EQUIPMENT/TOOLS
■	■
■	■
■	■
■	■

SIGHTINGS & ACTIVITY

FURTHER NOTES & OBSERVATIONS

LOCATION		DATE	
START TIME			
HUNTING TYPE		/	/

TEMPERATURE		WIND SPEED		
FLORA TYPE		WIND DIRECTION		

WEATHER CONDITION	☀ ☁ ❄ ⛈ 💨	TIME OF YEAR	🌷 ☀ 🍃 ❄

HOURS HUNTED	🕐	HUMIDITY	☀ / 💧
TIME CAUGHT			

TARGET SEX	⚥	TERRAIN LEVEL	1 2 3 4 5

HUNTING PARTY NAMES

WEAPONS/AMMO | EQUIPMENT/TOOLS

WEAPONS/AMMO	EQUIPMENT/TOOLS
■	■
■	■
■	■
■	■

SIGHTINGS & ACTIVITY

FURTHER NOTES & OBSERVATIONS

LOCATION			DATE	
START TIME				
HUNTING TYPE			/	/

TEMPERATURE			WIND SPEED							
FLORA TYPE			WIND DIRECTION							
WEATHER CONDITION	☀	☁	❄	⛈	≈	TIME OF YEAR	🌷	☀	🍂	❄
HOURS HUNTED	🕐					HUMIDITY	☀ / ◊			
TIME CAUGHT										
TARGET SEX	⚥					TERRAIN LEVEL	1	2	3	4	5

HUNTING PARTY NAMES

WEAPONS/AMMO	EQUIPMENT/TOOLS
■	■
■	■
■	■
■	■

SIGHTINGS & ACTIVITY

FURTHER NOTES & OBSERVATIONS

LOCATION		DATE	
START TIME			
HUNTING TYPE		/ /	

TEMPERATURE		WIND SPEED		
FLORA TYPE		WIND DIRECTION		

WEATHER CONDITION	☀ ☁ ❄ ⚡ 〜	TIME OF YEAR	🌷 ☀ 🍃 ❄

HOURS HUNTED	🕐	HUMIDITY	☀ / 💧
TIME CAUGHT			

TARGET SEX	⚥	TERRAIN LEVEL	1 2 3 4 5

HUNTING PARTY NAMES

WEAPONS/AMMO · EQUIPMENT/TOOLS

WEAPONS/AMMO	EQUIPMENT/TOOLS
▪	▪
▪	▪
▪	▪
▪	▪

SIGHTINGS & ACTIVITY

FURTHER NOTES & OBSERVATIONS

LOCATION		DATE	
START TIME			
HUNTING TYPE		/ /	

TEMPERATURE			WIND SPEED		
FLORA TYPE			WIND DIRECTION		

WEATHER CONDITION	☀ ☁ ❄ ⛈ 🌬	TIME OF YEAR	🌷 ☀ 🍂 ❄

HOURS HUNTED	🕐		HUMIDITY	
TIME CAUGHT				

TARGET SEX	⚥		TERRAIN LEVEL	1	2	3	4	5

HUNTING PARTY NAMES

WEAPONS/AMMO	EQUIPMENT/TOOLS
■	■
■	■
■	■
■	■

SIGHTINGS & ACTIVITY

FURTHER NOTES & OBSERVATIONS

LOCATION		DATE	
START TIME			
HUNTING TYPE		/ /	

TEMPERATURE		WIND SPEED	
FLORA TYPE		WIND DIRECTION	

WEATHER CONDITION	☀ ☁ ❄ ⛈ 💨	TIME OF YEAR	🌷 ☀ 🍂 ❄

HOURS HUNTED	⏱	HUMIDITY	☀ / 💧
TIME CAUGHT			

TARGET SEX	⚥	TERRAIN LEVEL	1 2 3 4 5

HUNTING PARTY NAMES

WEAPONS/AMMO | EQUIPMENT/TOOLS

WEAPONS/AMMO	EQUIPMENT/TOOLS
■	■
■	■
■	■
■	■

SIGHTINGS & ACTIVITY

FURTHER NOTES & OBSERVATIONS

LOCATION		DATE	
START TIME			
HUNTING TYPE		/ /	

TEMPERATURE		WIND SPEED	
FLORA TYPE		WIND DIRECTION	

WEATHER CONDITION	☀ ☁ ❄ ⛈ 💨	TIME OF YEAR	🌷 ☀ 🍂 ❄

HOURS HUNTED	🕐	HUMIDITY	☀/💧
TIME CAUGHT			

TARGET SEX	⚦	TERRAIN LEVEL	1 2 3 4 5

HUNTING PARTY NAMES

WEAPONS/AMMO | EQUIPMENT/TOOLS

WEAPONS/AMMO	EQUIPMENT/TOOLS
■	■
■	■
■	■
■	■

SIGHTINGS & ACTIVITY

FURTHER NOTES & OBSERVATIONS

LOCATION		DATE	
START TIME			
HUNTING TYPE		/ /	

TEMPERATURE		WIND SPEED	
FLORA TYPE		WIND DIRECTION	

WEATHER CONDITION	☀ ☁ ❄ ⛈ 🌬	TIME OF YEAR	🌷 ☀ 🍃 ❄

HOURS HUNTED	🕐	HUMIDITY	☀ / 💧
TIME CAUGHT			

TARGET SEX	⚥	TERRAIN LEVEL	1 2 3 4 5

HUNTING PARTY NAMES

WEAPONS/AMMO | ## EQUIPMENT/TOOLS

WEAPONS/AMMO	EQUIPMENT/TOOLS
■	■
■	■
■	■
■	■

SIGHTINGS & ACTIVITY

FURTHER NOTES & OBSERVATIONS

LOCATION						DATE		
START TIME								
HUNTING TYPE						/ /		

TEMPERATURE						WIND SPEED		
FLORA TYPE						WIND DIRECTION		
WEATHER CONDITION	☀	☁	❄	⛈	💨	TIME OF YEAR	🌷 ☀ 🍂 ❄	
HOURS HUNTED	🕐					HUMIDITY	☀/💧	
TIME CAUGHT								
TARGET SEX	⚥					TERRAIN LEVEL	1 2 3 4 5	

HUNTING PARTY NAMES

WEAPONS/AMMO | ## EQUIPMENT/TOOLS

WEAPONS/AMMO	EQUIPMENT/TOOLS
■	■
■	■
■	■
■	■

SIGHTINGS & ACTIVITY

FURTHER NOTES & OBSERVATIONS

LOCATION		DATE	
START TIME			
HUNTING TYPE		/ /	

TEMPERATURE		WIND SPEED		
FLORA TYPE		WIND DIRECTION		

WEATHER CONDITION	☀ ☁ ❄ ⛈ 💨	TIME OF YEAR	🌷 ☀ 🍃 ❄

HOURS HUNTED	🕐	HUMIDITY	
TIME CAUGHT			

TARGET SEX	⚥	TERRAIN LEVEL	1 2 3 4 5

HUNTING PARTY NAMES

WEAPONS/AMMO · EQUIPMENT/TOOLS

WEAPONS/AMMO	EQUIPMENT/TOOLS
■	■
■	■
■	■
■	■

SIGHTINGS & ACTIVITY

FURTHER NOTES & OBSERVATIONS

LOCATION		DATE	
START TIME			
HUNTING TYPE		/ /	

TEMPERATURE		WIND SPEED					
FLORA TYPE		WIND DIRECTION					
WEATHER CONDITION	☀ ☁ ❄ ⚡ 💨	TIME OF YEAR	🌷 ☀ 🍃 ❄				
HOURS HUNTED	🕐	HUMIDITY	☀ / 💧				
TIME CAUGHT							
TARGET SEX	⚥	TERRAIN LEVEL	1	2	3	4	5

HUNTING PARTY NAMES

WEAPONS/AMMO | EQUIPMENT/TOOLS

WEAPONS/AMMO	EQUIPMENT/TOOLS
■	■
■	■
■	■
■	■

SIGHTINGS & ACTIVITY

FURTHER NOTES & OBSERVATIONS

LOCATION		DATE	
START TIME			
HUNTING TYPE		/ /	

TEMPERATURE		WIND SPEED	
FLORA TYPE		WIND DIRECTION	

WEATHER CONDITION	☀ ☁ ❄ ⛈ 💨	TIME OF YEAR	🌷 ☀ 🍁 ❄

HOURS HUNTED		HUMIDITY	
TIME CAUGHT			

TARGET SEX	⚣	TERRAIN LEVEL	1 2 3 4 5

HUNTING PARTY NAMES

WEAPONS/AMMO | EQUIPMENT/TOOLS

WEAPONS/AMMO	EQUIPMENT/TOOLS
■	■
■	■
■	■
■	■

SIGHTINGS & ACTIVITY

FURTHER NOTES & OBSERVATIONS

LOCATION		DATE	
START TIME			
HUNTING TYPE		/ /	

TEMPERATURE		WIND SPEED		
FLORA TYPE		WIND DIRECTION		

WEATHER CONDITION	☀ ☁ ❄ ⛈ 🌬	TIME OF YEAR	🌷 ☀ 🍃 ❄

HOURS HUNTED	🕐	HUMIDITY	☀ / 💧
TIME CAUGHT			

TARGET SEX	⚥	TERRAIN LEVEL	1 2 3 4 5

HUNTING PARTY NAMES

WEAPONS/AMMO | EQUIPMENT/TOOLS

WEAPONS/AMMO	EQUIPMENT/TOOLS
■	■
■	■
■	■
■	■

SIGHTINGS & ACTIVITY

FURTHER NOTES & OBSERVATIONS

LOCATION		DATE	
START TIME			
HUNTING TYPE		/ /	

TEMPERATURE		WIND SPEED	
FLORA TYPE		WIND DIRECTION	

WEATHER CONDITION	☀ ☁ ❄ ⛈ 🌬	TIME OF YEAR	🌷 ☀ 🍃 ❄

HOURS HUNTED	🕐	HUMIDITY	☀ / 💧
TIME CAUGHT			

TARGET SEX	⚥	TERRAIN LEVEL	1 2 3 4 5

HUNTING PARTY NAMES

WEAPONS/AMMO / EQUIPMENT/TOOLS

■	■
■	■
■	■
■	■

SIGHTINGS & ACTIVITY

FURTHER NOTES & OBSERVATIONS

LOCATION		DATE	
START TIME			
HUNTING TYPE		/	/

TEMPERATURE		WIND SPEED		
FLORA TYPE		WIND DIRECTION		

WEATHER CONDITION	☀ ☁ ❄ ⛈ 💨	TIME OF YEAR	🌷 ☀ 🍂 ❄

HOURS HUNTED	🕐	HUMIDITY	☀ / 💧
TIME CAUGHT			

TARGET SEX	⚥	TERRAIN LEVEL	1 2 3 4 5

HUNTING PARTY NAMES

WEAPONS/AMMO · EQUIPMENT/TOOLS

WEAPONS/AMMO	EQUIPMENT/TOOLS
■	■
■	■
■	■
■	■

SIGHTINGS & ACTIVITY

FURTHER NOTES & OBSERVATIONS

LOCATION		DATE	
START TIME			
HUNTING TYPE		/ /	

TEMPERATURE		WIND SPEED	
FLORA TYPE		WIND DIRECTION	

WEATHER CONDITION	☀ ☁ ❄ ⛈ 💨	TIME OF YEAR	🌷 ☀ 🍃 ❄

HOURS HUNTED	🕐	HUMIDITY	☀ / 💧
TIME CAUGHT			

TARGET SEX	⚥	TERRAIN LEVEL	1 2 3 4 5

HUNTING PARTY NAMES

WEAPONS/AMMO · EQUIPMENT/TOOLS

WEAPONS/AMMO	EQUIPMENT/TOOLS
■	■
■	■
■	■
■	■

SIGHTINGS & ACTIVITY

FURTHER NOTES & OBSERVATIONS

LOCATION		DATE
START TIME		
HUNTING TYPE		/ /

TEMPERATURE		WIND SPEED		
FLORA TYPE		WIND DIRECTION		

WEATHER CONDITION	☀ ☁ ❄ ⛈ 🌬	TIME OF YEAR	🌷 ☀ 🍃 ❄

HOURS HUNTED	🕐	HUMIDITY	☀ / 💧
TIME CAUGHT			

TARGET SEX	⚥	TERRAIN LEVEL	1 2 3 4 5

HUNTING PARTY NAMES

WEAPONS/AMMO & EQUIPMENT/TOOLS

WEAPONS/AMMO	EQUIPMENT/TOOLS
■	■
■	■
■	■
■	■

SIGHTINGS & ACTIVITY

FURTHER NOTES & OBSERVATIONS

LOCATION		DATE	
START TIME			
HUNTING TYPE		/ /	

TEMPERATURE		WIND SPEED	⇌	
FLORA TYPE		WIND DIRECTION		

WEATHER CONDITION	☀ ☁ ❄ ⛈ ⇌	TIME OF YEAR	🌷 ☀ 🍂 ❄

HOURS HUNTED	🕐	HUMIDITY	☀ / 💧
TIME CAUGHT			

TARGET SEX	⚥	TERRAIN LEVEL	1 2 3 4 5

HUNTING PARTY NAMES

WEAPONS/AMMO · EQUIPMENT/TOOLS

WEAPONS/AMMO	EQUIPMENT/TOOLS
▪	▪
▪	▪
▪	▪
▪	▪

SIGHTINGS & ACTIVITY

FURTHER NOTES & OBSERVATIONS

LOCATION		DATE	
START TIME			
HUNTING TYPE		/ /	

TEMPERATURE		WIND SPEED		
FLORA TYPE		WIND DIRECTION		

WEATHER CONDITION	☀ ☁ ❄ ⛈ 💨	TIME OF YEAR	🌷 ☀ 🍂 ❄

HOURS HUNTED	🕐	HUMIDITY	
TIME CAUGHT			

TARGET SEX	⚥	TERRAIN LEVEL	1 2 3 4 5

HUNTING PARTY NAMES

WEAPONS/AMMO EQUIPMENT/TOOLS

■	■
■	■
■	■
■	■

SIGHTINGS & ACTIVITY

FURTHER NOTES & OBSERVATIONS

LOCATION		DATE	
START TIME			
HUNTING TYPE		/ /	

TEMPERATURE		WIND SPEED	
FLORA TYPE		WIND DIRECTION	

WEATHER CONDITION	☀ ☁ ❄ ⛈ 💨	TIME OF YEAR	🌷 ☀ 🍃 ❄

HOURS HUNTED	🕐	HUMIDITY	☀ / 💧
TIME CAUGHT			

TARGET SEX	⚥	TERRAIN LEVEL	1 2 3 4 5

HUNTING PARTY NAMES

WEAPONS/AMMO — EQUIPMENT/TOOLS

WEAPONS/AMMO	EQUIPMENT/TOOLS
■	■
■	■
■	■
■	■

SIGHTINGS & ACTIVITY

FURTHER NOTES & OBSERVATIONS

LOCATION		DATE	
START TIME			
HUNTING TYPE		/ /	

TEMPERATURE		WIND SPEED	⇌
FLORA TYPE		WIND DIRECTION	

WEATHER CONDITION	☀ ☁ ❄ ⛆ ⇌	TIME OF YEAR	❀ ☀ 🍂 ❄
HOURS HUNTED / TIME CAUGHT	🕐	HUMIDITY	☀ / 💧
TARGET SEX	⚥	TERRAIN LEVEL	1 2 3 4 5

HUNTING PARTY NAMES

WEAPONS/AMMO	EQUIPMENT/TOOLS
■	■
■	■
■	■
■	■

SIGHTINGS & ACTIVITY

FURTHER NOTES & OBSERVATIONS

LOCATION		DATE	
START TIME			
HUNTING TYPE		/ /	

TEMPERATURE		WIND SPEED	⇉	
FLORA TYPE		WIND DIRECTION		

WEATHER CONDITION	☀ ☁ ❄ ⛈ ⇉	TIME OF YEAR	🌷 ☀ 🍃 ❄

HOURS HUNTED	⏱	HUMIDITY	☀ / 💧
TIME CAUGHT			

TARGET SEX	⚥	TERRAIN LEVEL	1 2 3 4 5

HUNTING PARTY NAMES

WEAPONS/AMMO

EQUIPMENT/TOOLS

■	■
■	■
■	■
■	■

SIGHTINGS & ACTIVITY

FURTHER NOTES & OBSERVATIONS

LOCATION		DATE	
START TIME			
HUNTING TYPE		/ /	

TEMPERATURE		WIND SPEED	
FLORA TYPE		WIND DIRECTION	

WEATHER CONDITION	☀ ☁ ❄ ⛈ 💨	TIME OF YEAR	🌷 ☀ 🍃 ❄

HOURS HUNTED	🕐	HUMIDITY	☀ / 💧
TIME CAUGHT			

TARGET SEX	⚥	TERRAIN LEVEL	1 2 3 4 5

HUNTING PARTY NAMES

WEAPONS/AMMO · EQUIPMENT/TOOLS

WEAPONS/AMMO	EQUIPMENT/TOOLS
■	■
■	■
■	■
■	■

SIGHTINGS & ACTIVITY

FURTHER NOTES & OBSERVATIONS

LOCATION		DATE	
START TIME			
HUNTING TYPE		/ /	

TEMPERATURE				WIND SPEED	⇉						
FLORA TYPE				WIND DIRECTION							
WEATHER CONDITION	☀	☁	❄	⛈	⇉	TIME OF YEAR	🌷	☀	🍂	❄	
HOURS HUNTED	🕐			HUMIDITY	☀ / 💧						
TIME CAUGHT											
TARGET SEX	⚥			TERRAIN LEVEL	1	2	3	4	5		

HUNTING PARTY NAMES

WEAPONS/AMMO	EQUIPMENT/TOOLS
■	■
■	■
■	■
■	■

SIGHTINGS & ACTIVITY

FURTHER NOTES & OBSERVATIONS

LOCATION		DATE
START TIME		
HUNTING TYPE		/ /

TEMPERATURE		WIND SPEED	
FLORA TYPE		WIND DIRECTION	

WEATHER CONDITION	☀ 🌧 ❄ ⛈ 🌬	TIME OF YEAR	🌷 ☀ 🍃 ❄

HOURS HUNTED	🕐	HUMIDITY	☀ / 💧
TIME CAUGHT			

TARGET SEX	⚥	TERRAIN LEVEL	1 2 3 4 5

HUNTING PARTY NAMES

WEAPONS/AMMO · EQUIPMENT/TOOLS

WEAPONS/AMMO	EQUIPMENT/TOOLS
▪	▪
▪	▪
▪	▪
▪	▪

SIGHTINGS & ACTIVITY

FURTHER NOTES & OBSERVATIONS

LOCATION		DATE	
START TIME			
HUNTING TYPE		/	/

TEMPERATURE		WIND SPEED		
FLORA TYPE		WIND DIRECTION		

WEATHER CONDITION	☀ ☁ ❄ ⛈ 🌬	TIME OF YEAR	🌷 ☀ 🍃 ❄

HOURS HUNTED	🕐	HUMIDITY	☀ / 💧
TIME CAUGHT			

TARGET SEX	⚥	TERRAIN LEVEL	1 2 3 4 5

HUNTING PARTY NAMES

WEAPONS/AMMO   EQUIPMENT/TOOLS

■	■
■	■
■	■
■	■

SIGHTINGS & ACTIVITY

FURTHER NOTES & OBSERVATIONS

LOCATION		DATE		
START TIME				
HUNTING TYPE		/	/	

TEMPERATURE		WIND SPEED		
FLORA TYPE		WIND DIRECTION		

WEATHER CONDITION	☀ ☁ ❄ ⛈ 🌬	TIME OF YEAR	🌷 ☀ 🍂 ❄

HOURS HUNTED	🕐	HUMIDITY	☀ / 💧
TIME CAUGHT			

TARGET SEX	⚥	TERRAIN LEVEL	1 2 3 4 5

HUNTING PARTY NAMES

WEAPONS/AMMO | EQUIPMENT/TOOLS

WEAPONS/AMMO	EQUIPMENT/TOOLS
■	■
■	■
■	■
■	■

SIGHTINGS & ACTIVITY

FURTHER NOTES & OBSERVATIONS

LOCATION		DATE		
START TIME				
HUNTING TYPE		/	/	

TEMPERATURE		WIND SPEED		
FLORA TYPE		WIND DIRECTION		

WEATHER CONDITION	☀ ☁ ❄ ⛈ ≈	TIME OF YEAR	🌷 ☀ 🍃 ❄

HOURS HUNTED	🕐	HUMIDITY	☀ / 💧
TIME CAUGHT			

TARGET SEX	⚥	TERRAIN LEVEL	1 2 3 4 5

HUNTING PARTY NAMES

WEAPONS/AMMO · EQUIPMENT/TOOLS

WEAPONS/AMMO	EQUIPMENT/TOOLS
■	■
■	■
■	■
■	■

SIGHTINGS & ACTIVITY

FURTHER NOTES & OBSERVATIONS

LOCATION		DATE		
START TIME				
HUNTING TYPE		/ /		

TEMPERATURE			WIND SPEED	⇒	
FLORA TYPE			WIND DIRECTION		
WEATHER CONDITION	☀ ☁ ❄ ⛈ ⇒		TIME OF YEAR	🌷 ☀ 🍃 ❄	
HOURS HUNTED	🕐		HUMIDITY	☀ / 💧	
TIME CAUGHT					
TARGET SEX	⚥		TERRAIN LEVEL	1 2 3 4 5	

HUNTING PARTY NAMES

WEAPONS/AMMO | EQUIPMENT/TOOLS

WEAPONS/AMMO	EQUIPMENT/TOOLS
■	■
■	■
■	■
■	■

SIGHTINGS & ACTIVITY

FURTHER NOTES & OBSERVATIONS

LOCATION		DATE
START TIME		
HUNTING TYPE		/ /

TEMPERATURE		WIND SPEED		
FLORA TYPE		WIND DIRECTION		

WEATHER CONDITION	☀ ☁ ❄ ⛈ 🌬	TIME OF YEAR	🌷 ☀ 🍂 ❄

HOURS HUNTED	🕐	HUMIDITY	☀ / 💧
TIME CAUGHT			

TARGET SEX	⚥	TERRAIN LEVEL	1 2 3 4 5

HUNTING PARTY NAMES

WEAPONS/AMMO · EQUIPMENT/TOOLS

WEAPONS/AMMO	EQUIPMENT/TOOLS
■	■
■	■
■	■
■	■

SIGHTINGS & ACTIVITY

FURTHER NOTES & OBSERVATIONS

LOCATION		DATE	
START TIME			
HUNTING TYPE		/ /	

TEMPERATURE		WIND SPEED		
FLORA TYPE		WIND DIRECTION		

WEATHER CONDITION	☀ ☁ ❄ ⛈ 💨	TIME OF YEAR	🌷 ☀ 🍃 ❄

HOURS HUNTED	🕐	HUMIDITY	☀/💧
TIME CAUGHT			

TARGET SEX	⚥	TERRAIN LEVEL	1 2 3 4 5

HUNTING PARTY NAMES

WEAPONS/AMMO | EQUIPMENT/TOOLS

WEAPONS/AMMO	EQUIPMENT/TOOLS
■	■
■	■
■	■
■	■

SIGHTINGS & ACTIVITY

FURTHER NOTES & OBSERVATIONS

LOCATION		DATE
START TIME		
HUNTING TYPE		/ /

TEMPERATURE		WIND SPEED	
FLORA TYPE		WIND DIRECTION	

WEATHER CONDITION	☀ ☁ ❄ ⛈ 💨	TIME OF YEAR	🌷 ☀ 🍂 ❄

HOURS HUNTED	🕐	HUMIDITY	☀ / 💧
TIME CAUGHT			

TARGET SEX	⚥	TERRAIN LEVEL	1 2 3 4 5

HUNTING PARTY NAMES

WEAPONS/AMMO

EQUIPMENT/TOOLS

- ■
- ■
- ■
- ■

- ■
- ■
- ■
- ■

SIGHTINGS & ACTIVITY

FURTHER NOTES & OBSERVATIONS

LOCATION		DATE	
START TIME			
HUNTING TYPE		/ /	

TEMPERATURE		WIND SPEED	
FLORA TYPE		WIND DIRECTION	

WEATHER CONDITION	☀ ☁ ❄ ⚡ 🌬	TIME OF YEAR	🌷 ☀ 🍂 ❄

HOURS HUNTED	🕐	HUMIDITY	☀ / ◊
TIME CAUGHT			

TARGET SEX	⚥	TERRAIN LEVEL	1 2 3 4 5

HUNTING PARTY NAMES

WEAPONS/AMMO EQUIPMENT/TOOLS

■		■	
■		■	
■		■	
■		■	

SIGHTINGS & ACTIVITY

FURTHER NOTES & OBSERVATIONS

LOCATION		DATE	
START TIME			
HUNTING TYPE		/ /	

TEMPERATURE		WIND SPEED	
FLORA TYPE		WIND DIRECTION	

WEATHER CONDITION	☀ ☁ ❄ ⛈ 🌬	TIME OF YEAR	🌷 ☀ 🍃 ❄

HOURS HUNTED	🕐	HUMIDITY	☀ / 💧
TIME CAUGHT			

TARGET SEX	⚥	TERRAIN LEVEL	1 2 3 4 5

HUNTING PARTY NAMES

WEAPONS/AMMO · EQUIPMENT/TOOLS

WEAPONS/AMMO	EQUIPMENT/TOOLS
■	■
■	■
■	■
■	■

SIGHTINGS & ACTIVITY

FURTHER NOTES & OBSERVATIONS

LOCATION		DATE	
START TIME			
HUNTING TYPE		/ /	

TEMPERATURE		WIND SPEED	
FLORA TYPE		WIND DIRECTION	

WEATHER CONDITION	☀ ☁ ❄ ⛈ 🌬	TIME OF YEAR	🌷 ☀ 🍃 ❄

HOURS HUNTED	🕐	HUMIDITY	☀ / 💧
TIME CAUGHT			

TARGET SEX	⚥	TERRAIN LEVEL	1 2 3 4 5

HUNTING PARTY NAMES

WEAPONS/AMMO | ## EQUIPMENT/TOOLS

WEAPONS/AMMO	EQUIPMENT/TOOLS
■	■
■	■
■	■
■	■

SIGHTINGS & ACTIVITY

FURTHER NOTES & OBSERVATIONS

LOCATION		DATE	
START TIME			
HUNTING TYPE		/ /	

TEMPERATURE		WIND SPEED		
FLORA TYPE		WIND DIRECTION		
WEATHER CONDITION	☀ ☁ ❄ ⚡ 💨	TIME OF YEAR	🌷 ☀ 🍃 ❄	
HOURS HUNTED	🕐	HUMIDITY	☀ / 💧	
TIME CAUGHT				
TARGET SEX	⚥	TERRAIN LEVEL	1 2 3 4 5	

HUNTING PARTY NAMES

WEAPONS/AMMO | EQUIPMENT/TOOLS

WEAPONS/AMMO	EQUIPMENT/TOOLS
▪	▪
▪	▪
▪	▪
▪	▪

SIGHTINGS & ACTIVITY

FURTHER NOTES & OBSERVATIONS

LOCATION		DATE	
START TIME			
HUNTING TYPE		/ /	

TEMPERATURE		WIND SPEED		
FLORA TYPE		WIND DIRECTION		

WEATHER CONDITION	☀ ☁ ❄ ⛈ 🌬	TIME OF YEAR	🌷 ☀ 🍃 ❄

HOURS HUNTED	🕐	HUMIDITY	☀ / 💧
TIME CAUGHT			

TARGET SEX	⚥	TERRAIN LEVEL	1 2 3 4 5

HUNTING PARTY NAMES

WEAPONS/AMMO | EQUIPMENT/TOOLS

WEAPONS/AMMO	EQUIPMENT/TOOLS
■	■
■	■
■	■
■	■

SIGHTINGS & ACTIVITY

FURTHER NOTES & OBSERVATIONS

LOCATION		DATE	
START TIME			
HUNTING TYPE		/ /	

TEMPERATURE		WIND SPEED	
FLORA TYPE		WIND DIRECTION	

WEATHER CONDITION	☀ ☁ ❄ ⛈ 💨	TIME OF YEAR	🌷 ☀ 🍂 ❄

HOURS HUNTED	🕐	HUMIDITY	☀ / 💧
TIME CAUGHT			

TARGET SEX	⚥	TERRAIN LEVEL	1 2 3 4 5

HUNTING PARTY NAMES

WEAPONS/AMMO — EQUIPMENT/TOOLS

WEAPONS/AMMO	EQUIPMENT/TOOLS
▪	▪
▪	▪
▪	▪
▪	▪

SIGHTINGS & ACTIVITY

FURTHER NOTES & OBSERVATIONS

LOCATION		DATE	
START TIME			
HUNTING TYPE		/ /	

TEMPERATURE						WIND SPEED	〰				
FLORA TYPE						WIND DIRECTION					
WEATHER CONDITION	☀	☁	❄	⛈	〰	TIME OF YEAR	🌷	☀	🍁	❄	
HOURS HUNTED	🕐					HUMIDITY	☀ / water drop				
TIME CAUGHT											
TARGET SEX	♂♀					TERRAIN LEVEL	1	2	3	4	5

HUNTING PARTY NAMES

WEAPONS/AMMO	EQUIPMENT/TOOLS
■	■
■	■
■	■
■	■

SIGHTINGS & ACTIVITY

FURTHER NOTES & OBSERVATIONS

LOCATION		DATE		
START TIME				
HUNTING TYPE		/ /		

TEMPERATURE		WIND SPEED	
FLORA TYPE		WIND DIRECTION	

WEATHER CONDITION	☀ ☁ ❄ ⛈ 💨	TIME OF YEAR	🌷 ☀ 🍃 ❄

HOURS HUNTED	🕐	HUMIDITY	☀ / 💧
TIME CAUGHT			

TARGET SEX	⚥	TERRAIN LEVEL	1 2 3 4 5

HUNTING PARTY NAMES

WEAPONS/AMMO   EQUIPMENT/TOOLS

■	■
■	■
■	■
■	■

SIGHTINGS & ACTIVITY

FURTHER NOTES & OBSERVATIONS

LOCATION		DATE
START TIME		
HUNTING TYPE		/ /

TEMPERATURE						WIND SPEED		
FLORA TYPE						WIND DIRECTION		
WEATHER CONDITION	☀	☁	❄	⛈	💨	TIME OF YEAR	🌷 ☀ 🍃 ❄
HOURS HUNTED	🕐					HUMIDITY	☀/💧
TIME CAUGHT							
TARGET SEX	⚥					TERRAIN LEVEL	1 2 3 4 5

HUNTING PARTY NAMES

WEAPONS/AMMO	EQUIPMENT/TOOLS
■	■
■	■
■	■
■	■

SIGHTINGS & ACTIVITY

FURTHER NOTES & OBSERVATIONS

LOCATION		DATE	
START TIME			
HUNTING TYPE		/ /	

TEMPERATURE		WIND SPEED	
FLORA TYPE		WIND DIRECTION	

WEATHER CONDITION	☀ ☁ ❄ ⛈ 〰	TIME OF YEAR	🌷 ☀ 🍂 ❄

HOURS HUNTED	🕐	HUMIDITY	
TIME CAUGHT			

TARGET SEX	⚥	TERRAIN LEVEL	1 2 3 4 5

HUNTING PARTY NAMES

WEAPONS/AMMO

EQUIPMENT/TOOLS

- ■
- ■
- ■
- ■

- ■
- ■
- ■
- ■

SIGHTINGS & ACTIVITY

FURTHER NOTES & OBSERVATIONS

LOCATION		DATE	
START TIME			
HUNTING TYPE		/ /	

TEMPERATURE		WIND SPEED	
FLORA TYPE		WIND DIRECTION	

WEATHER CONDITION	☀ ☁ ❄ ⛈ 🌬	TIME OF YEAR	🌷 ☀ 🍃 ❄

HOURS HUNTED	🕐	HUMIDITY	☀ / 💧
TIME CAUGHT			

TARGET SEX	⚥	TERRAIN LEVEL	1 2 3 4 5

HUNTING PARTY NAMES

WEAPONS/AMMO | EQUIPMENT/TOOLS

WEAPONS/AMMO	EQUIPMENT/TOOLS
■	■
■	■
■	■
■	■

SIGHTINGS & ACTIVITY

FURTHER NOTES & OBSERVATIONS

LOCATION		DATE	
START TIME			
HUNTING TYPE		/ /	

TEMPERATURE						WIND SPEED				
FLORA TYPE						WIND DIRECTION				
WEATHER CONDITION	☀	☁	❄	⛈	〜	TIME OF YEAR	❀	☀	🍂	❄
HOURS HUNTED	🕐					HUMIDITY	☀ / 💧			
TIME CAUGHT										
TARGET SEX	⚥					TERRAIN LEVEL	1	2	3	4 5

HUNTING PARTY NAMES

WEAPONS/AMMO | EQUIPMENT/TOOLS

WEAPONS/AMMO	EQUIPMENT/TOOLS
■	■
■	■
■	■
■	■

SIGHTINGS & ACTIVITY

FURTHER NOTES & OBSERVATIONS

LOCATION		DATE		
START TIME				
HUNTING TYPE		/ /		

TEMPERATURE		WIND SPEED		
FLORA TYPE		WIND DIRECTION		
WEATHER CONDITION	☀ ☁ ❄ ⛈ 🌬	TIME OF YEAR	🌷 ☀ 🍁 ❄	
HOURS HUNTED	🕐	HUMIDITY	☀ / 💧	
TIME CAUGHT				
TARGET SEX	⚥	TERRAIN LEVEL	1 2 3 4 5	

HUNTING PARTY NAMES

WEAPONS/AMMO | EQUIPMENT/TOOLS

WEAPONS/AMMO	EQUIPMENT/TOOLS
■	■
■	■
■	■
■	■

SIGHTINGS & ACTIVITY

FURTHER NOTES & OBSERVATIONS

LOCATION		DATE
START TIME		
HUNTING TYPE		/ /

TEMPERATURE		WIND SPEED		
FLORA TYPE		WIND DIRECTION		
WEATHER CONDITION	☀ ☁ ❄ ⛈ 💨	TIME OF YEAR	🌷 ☀ 🍂 ❄
HOURS HUNTED	🕐	HUMIDITY	☀ / 💧
TIME CAUGHT			
TARGET SEX	⚥	TERRAIN LEVEL	1 2 3 4 5

HUNTING PARTY NAMES

WEAPONS/AMMO

EQUIPMENT/TOOLS

WEAPONS/AMMO	EQUIPMENT/TOOLS
■	■
■	■
■	■
■	■

SIGHTINGS & ACTIVITY

FURTHER NOTES & OBSERVATIONS

LOCATION		DATE
START TIME		
HUNTING TYPE		/ /

TEMPERATURE		WIND SPEED	
FLORA TYPE		WIND DIRECTION	

WEATHER CONDITION	☀ ☁ ❄ ⛈ 💨	TIME OF YEAR	🌷 ☀ 🍃 ❄

HOURS HUNTED	🕐	HUMIDITY	☀ / 💧
TIME CAUGHT			

TARGET SEX	⚥	TERRAIN LEVEL	1 2 3 4 5

HUNTING PARTY NAMES

WEAPONS/AMMO · EQUIPMENT/TOOLS

▪	▪
▪	▪
▪	▪
▪	▪

SIGHTINGS & ACTIVITY

FURTHER NOTES & OBSERVATIONS

LOCATION		DATE
START TIME		
HUNTING TYPE		/ /

TEMPERATURE		WIND SPEED		
FLORA TYPE		WIND DIRECTION		

WEATHER CONDITION	☀ ☁ ❄ ⛈ 💨	TIME OF YEAR	🌷 ☀ 🍂 ❄

HOURS HUNTED	🕐	HUMIDITY	☀ / 💧
TIME CAUGHT			

TARGET SEX	⚥	TERRAIN LEVEL	1 2 3 4 5

HUNTING PARTY NAMES

WEAPONS/AMMO | EQUIPMENT/TOOLS

WEAPONS/AMMO	EQUIPMENT/TOOLS
■	■
■	■
■	■
■	■

SIGHTINGS & ACTIVITY

FURTHER NOTES & OBSERVATIONS

LOCATION		DATE
START TIME		
HUNTING TYPE		/ /

TEMPERATURE		WIND SPEED		
FLORA TYPE		WIND DIRECTION		

WEATHER CONDITION	☀ ☁ ❄ ⛈ 🌬	TIME OF YEAR	🌷 ☀ 🍂 ❄

HOURS HUNTED	🕐	HUMIDITY	☀ / 💧
TIME CAUGHT			

TARGET SEX	⚥	TERRAIN LEVEL	1 2 3 4 5

HUNTING PARTY NAMES

WEAPONS/AMMO | EQUIPMENT/TOOLS

■	■
■	■
■	■
■	■

SIGHTINGS & ACTIVITY

FURTHER NOTES & OBSERVATIONS

LOCATION		DATE	
START TIME			
HUNTING TYPE		/ /	

TEMPERATURE		WIND SPEED	
FLORA TYPE		WIND DIRECTION	

WEATHER CONDITION	☀ ☁ ❄ ⛈ 🌬	TIME OF YEAR	🌷 ☀ 🍂 ❄

HOURS HUNTED	🕐	HUMIDITY	☀ / 💧
TIME CAUGHT			

TARGET SEX	⚥	TERRAIN LEVEL	1 2 3 4 5

HUNTING PARTY NAMES

WEAPONS/AMMO | EQUIPMENT/TOOLS

WEAPONS/AMMO	EQUIPMENT/TOOLS
■	■
■	■
■	■
■	■

SIGHTINGS & ACTIVITY

FURTHER NOTES & OBSERVATIONS

LOCATION		DATE
START TIME		
HUNTING TYPE		/ /

TEMPERATURE		WIND SPEED		
FLORA TYPE		WIND DIRECTION		

WEATHER CONDITION	☀ ☁ ❄ ⛈ 🌬	TIME OF YEAR	🌷 ☀ 🍁 ❄

HOURS HUNTED	🕐	HUMIDITY	☀ / 💧
TIME CAUGHT			

TARGET SEX	⚥	TERRAIN LEVEL	1 2 3 4 5

HUNTING PARTY NAMES

WEAPONS/AMMO · EQUIPMENT/TOOLS

■	■
■	■
■	■
■	■

SIGHTINGS & ACTIVITY

FURTHER NOTES & OBSERVATIONS

LOCATION		DATE	
START TIME			
HUNTING TYPE		/ /	

TEMPERATURE		WIND SPEED	
FLORA TYPE		WIND DIRECTION	

WEATHER CONDITION	☀ ☁ ❄ ⛈ 🌬	TIME OF YEAR	🌷 ☀ 🍁 ❄

HOURS HUNTED	🕐	HUMIDITY	☀ / 💧
TIME CAUGHT			

TARGET SEX	⚥	TERRAIN LEVEL	1　2　3　4　5

HUNTING PARTY NAMES

WEAPONS/AMMO · EQUIPMENT/TOOLS

WEAPONS/AMMO	EQUIPMENT/TOOLS
▪	▪
▪	▪
▪	▪
▪	▪

SIGHTINGS & ACTIVITY

FURTHER NOTES & OBSERVATIONS

LOCATION		DATE	
START TIME			
HUNTING TYPE		/ /	

TEMPERATURE			WIND SPEED	⇌	
FLORA TYPE			WIND DIRECTION		

WEATHER CONDITION	☼ ☁ ❄ ⛈ ⇌		TIME OF YEAR	🌷 ☼ 🍃 ❄	

HOURS HUNTED	🕐		HUMIDITY	☼/💧	
TIME CAUGHT					

TARGET SEX	⚥		TERRAIN LEVEL	1 2 3 4 5	

HUNTING PARTY NAMES

WEAPONS/AMMO | ## EQUIPMENT/TOOLS

■	■
■	■
■	■
■	■

SIGHTINGS & ACTIVITY

FURTHER NOTES & OBSERVATIONS

LOCATION		DATE
START TIME		
HUNTING TYPE		/ /

TEMPERATURE		WIND SPEED	
FLORA TYPE		WIND DIRECTION	

WEATHER CONDITION	☀ ☁ ❄ ⛈ 〰	TIME OF YEAR	🌷 ☀ 🍂 ❄

HOURS HUNTED		HUMIDITY	
TIME CAUGHT			

TARGET SEX	⚥	TERRAIN LEVEL	1 2 3 4 5

HUNTING PARTY NAMES

WEAPONS/AMMO — EQUIPMENT/TOOLS

WEAPONS/AMMO	EQUIPMENT/TOOLS
■	■
■	■
■	■
■	■

SIGHTINGS & ACTIVITY

FURTHER NOTES & OBSERVATIONS

LOCATION		DATE	
START TIME			
HUNTING TYPE		/ /	

TEMPERATURE		WIND SPEED	
FLORA TYPE		WIND DIRECTION	

WEATHER CONDITION	☀ ☁ ❄ ⛈ 🌬	TIME OF YEAR	🌷 ☀ 🍂 ❄

HOURS HUNTED	🕐	HUMIDITY	☀ / 💧
TIME CAUGHT			

TARGET SEX	⚥	TERRAIN LEVEL	1 2 3 4 5

HUNTING PARTY NAMES

WEAPONS/AMMO / EQUIPMENT/TOOLS

■	■
■	■
■	■
■	■

SIGHTINGS & ACTIVITY

FURTHER NOTES & OBSERVATIONS

LOCATION		DATE	
START TIME			
HUNTING TYPE		/ /	

TEMPERATURE		WIND SPEED	
FLORA TYPE		WIND DIRECTION	

WEATHER CONDITION	☀ ☁ ❄ ⛈ 〰	TIME OF YEAR	🌷 ☀ 🍃 ❄

HOURS HUNTED		HUMIDITY	
TIME CAUGHT			

TARGET SEX	⚥	TERRAIN LEVEL	1 2 3 4 5

HUNTING PARTY NAMES

WEAPONS/AMMO	EQUIPMENT/TOOLS
■	■
■	■
■	■
■	■

SIGHTINGS & ACTIVITY

FURTHER NOTES & OBSERVATIONS

LOCATION		DATE	
START TIME			
HUNTING TYPE		/ /	

TEMPERATURE		WIND SPEED	⇒	
FLORA TYPE		WIND DIRECTION		

WEATHER CONDITION	☀ ☁ ❄ ⛈ ⇒	TIME OF YEAR	🌷 ☀ 🍂 ❄

HOURS HUNTED	🕐	HUMIDITY	☀ / ○
TIME CAUGHT			

TARGET SEX	⚥	TERRAIN LEVEL	1 2 3 4 5

HUNTING PARTY NAMES

WEAPONS/AMMO / EQUIPMENT/TOOLS

WEAPONS/AMMO	EQUIPMENT/TOOLS
■	■
■	■
■	■
■	■

SIGHTINGS & ACTIVITY

FURTHER NOTES & OBSERVATIONS

LOCATION		DATE	
START TIME			
HUNTING TYPE		/ /	

TEMPERATURE		WIND SPEED		
FLORA TYPE		WIND DIRECTION		

WEATHER CONDITION	☀ ☁ ❄ ⛈ 🌬	TIME OF YEAR	🌷 ☀ 🍁 ❄

HOURS HUNTED	🕐	HUMIDITY	☀ / 💧
TIME CAUGHT			

TARGET SEX	⚥	TERRAIN LEVEL	1 2 3 4 5

HUNTING PARTY NAMES

WEAPONS/AMMO & EQUIPMENT/TOOLS

WEAPONS/AMMO	EQUIPMENT/TOOLS
■	■
■	■
■	■
■	■

SIGHTINGS & ACTIVITY

FURTHER NOTES & OBSERVATIONS

LOCATION		DATE
START TIME		
HUNTING TYPE		/ /

TEMPERATURE		WIND SPEED	
FLORA TYPE		WIND DIRECTION	

WEATHER CONDITION	☀ ☁ ❄ ⛈ 🌬	TIME OF YEAR	🌷 ☀ 🍃 ❄

HOURS HUNTED	🕐	HUMIDITY	☀ / 💧
TIME CAUGHT			

TARGET SEX	⚥	TERRAIN LEVEL	1 2 3 4 5

HUNTING PARTY NAMES

WEAPONS/AMMO | EQUIPMENT/TOOLS

WEAPONS/AMMO	EQUIPMENT/TOOLS
■	■
■	■
■	■
■	■

SIGHTINGS & ACTIVITY

FURTHER NOTES & OBSERVATIONS

LOCATION		DATE	
START TIME			
HUNTING TYPE		/ /	

TEMPERATURE		WIND SPEED		
FLORA TYPE		WIND DIRECTION		

WEATHER CONDITION	☀ ☁ ❄ ⛈ ≋	TIME OF YEAR	🌷 ☀ 🍃 ❄

HOURS HUNTED	🕐	HUMIDITY	☀ / 💧
TIME CAUGHT			

TARGET SEX	⚥	TERRAIN LEVEL	1 2 3 4 5

HUNTING PARTY NAMES

WEAPONS/AMMO — EQUIPMENT/TOOLS

■	■
■	■
■	■
■	■

SIGHTINGS & ACTIVITY

FURTHER NOTES & OBSERVATIONS

LOCATION		DATE	
START TIME			
HUNTING TYPE		/ /	

TEMPERATURE		WIND SPEED	
FLORA TYPE		WIND DIRECTION	

WEATHER CONDITION	☀ ☁ ❄ ⛈ 💨	TIME OF YEAR	🌷 ☀ 🍃 ❄

HOURS HUNTED	🕐	HUMIDITY	
TIME CAUGHT			

TARGET SEX	⚥	TERRAIN LEVEL	1 2 3 4 5

HUNTING PARTY NAMES

WEAPONS/AMMO | EQUIPMENT/TOOLS

WEAPONS/AMMO	EQUIPMENT/TOOLS
■	■
■	■
■	■
■	■

SIGHTINGS & ACTIVITY

FURTHER NOTES & OBSERVATIONS

LOCATION		DATE	
START TIME			
HUNTING TYPE		/ /	

TEMPERATURE		WIND SPEED	
FLORA TYPE		WIND DIRECTION	

WEATHER CONDITION	☀ ☁ ❄ ⛈ 💨	TIME OF YEAR	🌷 ☀ 🍁 ❄

HOURS HUNTED	🕐	HUMIDITY	☀ / 💧
TIME CAUGHT			

TARGET SEX	⚥	TERRAIN LEVEL	1 2 3 4 5

HUNTING PARTY NAMES

WEAPONS/AMMO | ## EQUIPMENT/TOOLS

WEAPONS/AMMO	EQUIPMENT/TOOLS
■	■
■	■
■	■
■	■

SIGHTINGS & ACTIVITY

FURTHER NOTES & OBSERVATIONS

LOCATION		DATE	
START TIME			
HUNTING TYPE		/ /	

TEMPERATURE		WIND SPEED		
FLORA TYPE		WIND DIRECTION		

WEATHER CONDITION	☀ ☁ ❄ ⛈ 〰	TIME OF YEAR	🌷 ☀ 🍂 ❄

HOURS HUNTED	🕐	HUMIDITY	☀ / 💧
TIME CAUGHT			

TARGET SEX	⚥	TERRAIN LEVEL	1 2 3 4 5

HUNTING PARTY NAMES

WEAPONS/AMMO · EQUIPMENT/TOOLS

WEAPONS/AMMO	EQUIPMENT/TOOLS
■	■
■	■
■	■
■	■

SIGHTINGS & ACTIVITY

FURTHER NOTES & OBSERVATIONS

LOCATION		DATE
START TIME		
HUNTING TYPE		/ /

TEMPERATURE		WIND SPEED	
FLORA TYPE		WIND DIRECTION	

WEATHER CONDITION	☀ ☁ ❄ ⛈ 🌬	TIME OF YEAR	🌷 ☀ 🍂 ❄

HOURS HUNTED	🕐	HUMIDITY	☀ / 💧
TIME CAUGHT			

TARGET SEX	⚥	TERRAIN LEVEL	1 2 3 4 5

HUNTING PARTY NAMES

WEAPONS/AMMO

EQUIPMENT/TOOLS

- ▪
- ▪
- ▪
- ▪

- ▪
- ▪
- ▪
- ▪

SIGHTINGS & ACTIVITY

FURTHER NOTES & OBSERVATIONS

Thanks For Reading!

Just a quick message to thank you so much for picking up one of our books! Our sincere hope is that this book has given you the value we always look to provide, and hope we can continue to produce quality books that will in anyway contribute to a better quality of life for our readers.

We are a small independent publisher based in London, UK and we work with talented authors from around the world, who dedicate every ounce of their effort to craft these memorable books for your reading pleasure.

The author of this title would love to hear about your experience with the book, and your review will go a long way to provide them with the insight and encouragement they need to keep creating the kind of books you want to read.

<u>Your Opinion Makes a Real Difference.</u>

If you want to let us know what you thought about the book, please visit the Amazon website and give us your review. We read every single review, no matter how long or short!

HAPPY READING!

MOONPEAK™

PUBLISHERS

Made in the USA
Las Vegas, NV
19 November 2024